THE ENTREPRENEUR'S GRAVEYARD

CISLYN DEEN BROWN

THE ENTREPRENEUR'S GRAVEYARD

By Cislyn Deen Brown

Copyright © 2022
ALL RIGHTS RESERVED

Unless otherwise indicated, all scripture quotations are taken for the King James Version of the Bible

FOR MORE INFORMATION
CONTACT

Cislyn Brown
cislynbooks@yahoo.com
(301) 537-4764

Online ordering is available for all products

Dedication Page

This book is dedicated to all of the hard working, self-motivated, curious, proactive and creative visionaries. You have always had a burning desire for entrepreneurial pursuit; but, somehow you find yourself being the helpmate to someone else's dream longer than you intended. Nevertheless, you continue to feel the tugging of your calling on your heart and the undying desire for more. I hope this book will ignite something inside of you to finish what you've started, get up and start again, and exceed your own expectations.

FOREWORD

Doing what you have to do and doing what you love to do, or what you have been called to do for most people, are two conflicting pulls. This book is an excellent eye opener and encouragement to those who struggle with these conflicts and will help you to make the decision to refuse to die without pursuing your God-given dreams; refusing to make the graveyard, the place where many hopes and dreams were never fulfilled, any richer.

I have known the author for most of her life. She always possessed an entrepreneurial spirit. For more than 25 years, I have watched her served passionately and selflessly from the heart as she gave her time and talent as a gifted mental health clinician, impacting and transforming lives in numerous mental health institutions, group homes and hospitals.

However, deep within her there was always a deep passion to pursue her entrepreneurial dream. Today I am extremely proud of her determination for taking the leap of faith to step out of the comfort zone of the 9-5 or employment (the graveyard) to pursue her dreams and to fulfill her destiny as an entrepreneur. She has written this book to share her journey and to encourage everyone with an entrepreneurial spirit to develop the courage to get out of the graveyard to pursue their entrepreneurial dream as well.

This book is a must read. It is an inspiration to everyone who may be at the crossroad of complacency and the fulfillment of your destiny. This book will help you overcome your doubts, fears, and insecurities. It will help you to gather the guts to fulfill your dream by taking a leap of faith.

The entrepreneur's Graveyard will challenge you, not to bury your talent, or be buried with your talent. You will be challenged to get out of the graveyard and live your best life and fulfill your destiny. Stop settling or looking for your dream job and start building your dream life.

Dr. Jasmin Brown

Table of Contents

INTRODUCTION

Lately, I have been thinking a lot about the late Dr. Myles Monroe who said; "The wealthiest places in the world are not the gold mines of South America or the oil fields of Iraq or Iran. They are not even the diamond mines of South Africa or the banks of the world. The wealthiest place on the planet is just down the road. It is the cemetery. There lie buried companies that were never started, inventions that were never made, bestselling books that were never written, and masterpieces that were never painted. In the cemetery is buried the greatest treasure of untapped potential."

Like many of you, I have always been very ambitious, motivated and energetic; yet, I have never been able to fit in any mold. I am human, so this sense of being a misfit often brought me to tears and caused me to question my sense of belonging. Consequently, in an attempt to feel accomplished, over the years, I have worked many jobs where I've taken pride in going above and beyond to serve my employers, my staff, my clients and my patients. I routinely worked harder and stayed longer than everyone else. I continuously contributed to organizational expansion and the financial growth of many businesses, while only being paid a menial wage as an employee.

Months turned into years as I watched the rise and fall of several individuals, and listened to the "would have and could have" stories of many others along the way. While I've experienced promotions and monetary compensations, I have never felt fulfilled. This emptiness kept me hungry for more, and continued to push me to examine my life; each time coming up with more questions than answers.

With a deep unwillingness to become complacent, I had to confront my own truth. I could no longer deny the truth that I had been burying my dreams alive in order to "survive". This painful truth overshadowed me with sadness when I realized I was burying my dreams to not even swore among eagles; but, to merely be mediocre and maneuver among the crowded and overly populated masses. This awareness motivated me in acting to incorporate my business ideas and further created the steps aimed at moving me from stagnation to realization. Additionally, I began to evaluate the series of events that led me through those lost moments that quickly became lost years.

Hence, the intent of this book is to serve as a relatable tool that will ignite every sleeping giant to rise up, provoke every builder, writer, singer, inventor and creator to do try again. So, regardless of where you are on your journey, may this book be an inspiration for you to go farther than you have been and eventually to become the best version of yourself.

Letter to My Entrepreneur Self

Dear Self,

I know the journey to the present has been long, hard, and sometimes confusing. However, because of how you are wired, you had to walk the lonesome valley, you had to do it your way and I know it's been painful. But, I've been there with you the entire time. I've seen the disappointments in your eyes and felt the pain in your heart as you try to figure out why you can't fit in. I heard your questions about why you think differently and although you have always worked harder at every job; yet, like Goldilocks, things never feel right.

Hey, I was there with you when it was all a dream and you were bursting with excitement everywhere. I also remember when you shared your dreams with a few dream-snatchers and you cried because it appeared they stole your idea. I also know about the doubts and insecurity you carry because you started and failed so many times and for all of that I am sorry.

I am sorry that you don't know how strong and powerful you really are. I am also sorry that you fail to realize that the things that were meant to kill you were really employed to develop resilience and fortitude. These valuable assets, and life-sustaining attributes are the things that money cannot acquire; instead, they are rather cultivated only on a personal journey. I am saddened by the fact that cannot see yourself like I see you or even as your so-called enemies see you. But, I'm so happy you have not given up. Tried but not tired, frustrated but not bitter, bruised but not broken in despair.

I just want to tell you that it looks good. Yes, your end, it looks good. So, get ready to level-up because it's time. They've been waiting to meet you. The assignments are ready for distribution and you are the only one who has been given these particular assignments and the necessary skills set to accomplish them. You are ready and persons are rooting for you. You are loved and always surrounded by those who love you so you are never alone. Remember, you were sent here for this and now it is time. So, let's go!

CHAPTER ONE

THE BIRTHING

In the beginning it was only a great idea, then without warning, this idea began to take form in the mind. Minutes began turning into hours, and hours began turning into days as I effortlessly found myself researching about this idea. It was unbeknown to me that there were sparkles in my eyes, and emphasis in my diction as I was sharing this idea with family and close friends. Before long, I found myself evaluating the pros and the cons of executing this idea. But, inevitably, I identified far more benefits than drawbacks; and so, this idea became one with my being.

Over time, this idea crept itself into every one conversation, consumed my mind; and, before I knew it, I became dedicated to this idea. Needless to say, I wanted this idea materialized more than anything else. Propelled by this overwhelming desire, with much enthusiasm, I was compelled to act in order to transition from potentiality into actuality. Passion was developed and I began exploring the process of birthing this idea into a tangible form, exploring the resources needed and how to access these resources. Before long, I began to play with the thought that this could be the best route to financial freedom and to building generational wealth. However, passion met with uncertainty and fear, while waiting to have an encounter with opportunity.

At this point, something internal continued motivating me to move forward, do more, and pursue this new assignment with unwavering faith. Even without the full manifestation of the dream, I embraced the internal transformation and began to refer to myself as a CEO. Throughout the years, I would encourage myself by reflecting on my previous publication; wherein I discussed the significance of the CEO remaining mindful of the organization's mission and ultimate purpose for existing.

This personal reflection was done constantly simply because I saw myself as a CEO in my mind, and so I remained conscious of the greater purpose behind my day to day maneuver, I put my mission in writing and created long term and short-term goals in order to enhance my focus on my mission daily. In fact, I created vision boards and placed them in multiple places that were visible.

One thing I knew for sure, was that no matter what my employment status was, I always saw myself as the CEO of my own establishment in the now and not just in the future. With this consciousness, I began to identify business concepts such as my audience and target population, product/service and financial plan. Additionally, I found myself signing up for work-shops, seminars and trainings to enhance my natural abilities while learning new skills needed to succeed at my new endeavors. At this significant junction in my life, my professional appetite has begun to develop as I yearned to communicate and interact with more like-minded people. A birthing has taken place as I began to refer to myself as an ENTREPRENEUR.

CHAPTER TWO

THE MEETING AT THE CROSSROAD

Even with all of the enthusiasm of birthing another dimension of myself, I recognized that there is a critical junction where a decision is made consciously or unconsciously. A decision made to either pursue the entrepreneurial path or to pursue the perceived safe and stable path, (also known as secured employment). Clouded by uncertainty, lack of resources and endless unfavorable situations, many of us continuously make the decision to remain employed and pursue the entrepreneurial goals "on the side".

In essence, at this junction, like most new entrepreneurs, we contemplate the consequences of strategic turns (C.O.S.T). Without any verbal expressions, we find ourselves counting the C.O.S.T of required time, the financial C.O.S.T, or the C.O.S.T of undergoing the transformation of becoming a successful entrepreneur. In fact, this is the junction where we negotiate the C.O.S.T of instant gratifications versus the C.O.S.T of delayed gratifications.

This is the junction where a battle is often waged among secured employment, the deep tugging to take the leap of faith to pursue the path of entrepreneurship relentlessly, mountains of fear, lack of trust and an unimaginable amount of "what ifs".   Sadly, this is also the intersection where traumatic experiences may hold us hostage without a gun and inoculate us with mental paralytics. Consequently, it may become impossible to see the glory that exists beyond the challenges in the immediate view on the entrepreneurial path. Thus, with or without intention, a decision is always made to exit the crossroad because no-one stays at a crossroad forever.

CHAPTER THREE

THE JOURNEY TO THE ENTREPRENEUR'S GRAVEYARD

For many with entrepreneurial dreams, ashes to ashes and dust to dust was pronounced over our hopes and dreams as the extermination of our books, songs, and inventions was carried out long before the mortal body is laid to rest. The devastating reality is that there are too many entrepreneurs who continue to bury the heartbeat of our passion, the path to financial freedom and the unseen possibilities of our destiny. I now realize that without a definitive decision at the crossroad, I became involved in a "side-chick" relationship with my passion immediately after I exited the crossroad.

Erroneously, I had convinced myself that I hadn't given up on my passion because at least I still had a "side-chick" relationship with my dreams. But, like most "side-chicks", my passion gave me excitement, and provided an escape from the stressors that I often experienced at the very thing I chose instead of pursuing my entrepreneurial dream. However, this "side-chick" relationship with my passion also meant I was less committed or devoted, causing me to spent minimal time doing the things that would have strengthen the potential for growth and success of my entrepreneurial desire.

In hind-sight, I now realize that I embarked on the journey to the entrepreneur's graveyard the moment I exited the crossroad and I began creating multiple resumes to compliment my job search, instead of creating plans to fund my entrepreneurial dream. Thus, I continue to ask myself if I've surrendered to the invisible force that influences many entrepreneurs to voluntarily bury such great calling to serve humanity, change the trajectory of their lives and/or create generational wealth. Yet, could it be that there are many of us whose entrepreneurial dreams haven't died just yet. They are still there waiting to be materialized as we struggle to remain professionally optimistic with an employer while fantasizing about our entrepreneurial goals.

Nevertheless, I am aware that there are many people who have counted the C.O.S.T and simply made a conscious decision to take the path that most persons have traveled. However, the longer I remained at the entrepreneur's graveyard, the more I was confronted with the realization that I'd become a back-seat driver in my own life. Like a real back -seat driver, I have always had all of the necessary pre-requisites to sit and function well in the driver's seat. I am equipped with the skills to drive and know all the right turns to take. Yet, I don't control the steering wheel and he who controls the wheels controls the moves and direction on the journey.

CHAPTER FOUR

THE UnEQuAL Trade Transaction

Like many entrepreneurs, I entered the entrepreneur's graveyard with the best intentions for it to be a means to an end, a temporary situation, revenue to cover immediate financial obligations, or a place to serve "until the business takes off". Soon, temporary became extended, the means became the end and the only business that kept taking off were the ones I found myself serving. The fascinating yet distorted promises of a steady and secured stream of income was only assassinating the dream of entrepreneurship.

I was young, ambitious and energetic when I arrived at my first graveyard. Being naïve, I shared my dream of one day becoming an entrepreneur with a coworker I believed to be a friend. This coworker shared my dream with the CEO who terminated me on the premise of "conflict of interest". At that time, it was only a dream. I had no money, no article of incorporation, only a dream. Not only did they terminated me; but, they fought and blocked me from collecting unemployment. Needless to say, I lost everything and struggled for a substantial period of time to regain stability.

I continued to ask myself what were they afraid of, and how could an established company have terminated someone with nothing because they had a dream? Of course, there were some fabrications about me having the intention of taking away all of their staff and other unrealistic stories attached. If only they had known that even then, I had no intention of remaining in the same state. So, the truth is that it was only a dream and remained a dream for many years to come. But, even then I knew I wanted to be an agent of change, a trailblazer and a community leader.

I can still remember that morning when the unemployment office called at 9:00 a.m. and an inner impression said "don't you get on that phone and put in the atmosphere that you don't own a business". I battled with that internal impression and said out loud "but I need the money". But the inner voice was unwavering and kept insisting; "don't you declare in the atmosphere that you don't have a business". I battled until the phone stopped ringing. Needless to say, I did not collect my unemployment and I also did not succeed at my first or even my second attempt at entrepreneurship; thus, finding myself at several other graveyards throughout the years to come.

Reflecting back on fifteen (15) years ago when I met an energetic fifty-five (55) years old lady who had been at the same graveyard for twenty-two (22) years. On numerous occasions she had shared her story about wanting to create an amazing Bed & Breakfast in North Carolina. She described the southern meals that she wanted to provide and became overjoyed as she described the details of the hospitality and charm that she wanted all of her guests to experience. One day I became inquisitive and asked her why she never pursued her dreams that seemed to be so alive in her heart even then. To my dismay, she replied, "life just happened". She continued to inform me that she only had few more years left to retire and had decided to remain at the entrepreneur's graveyard for the remainder of her time. In that moment she attempted to convince me that she was contented with her decision to trade her passion for a position. I became frightened by her story and fled while I still had a pulse; only to find myself at yet another entrepreneur's graveyard.

This was where I witnessed another unequal life transaction, wherein a thirty-nine (39) years old woman from New Orleans traded her passion to have her own private practice for a promotion. She would explain how she is only at the graveyard to make money to pay her rent at her practice in the future. I would say to her, "do you realize two new clients per week could pay your rent?". She could never fathom the fact that for as long as she is investing all her time at the graveyard, she will never have time for her practice. Well, sadly she remained at the graveyard with an amazing dream to counsel children who were victims of sex trafficking. I often wondered how many broken children suffered because she buried her dreams alive.

After years of wandering from one graveyard to the next I am reminded of Genesis 37 verse 15 that states:

> "Now a certain man found Joseph, and saw that he was wandering around and had lost his way in the field; so, the man asked him, "What are you looking for?"

So, I began asking myself, what are we all looking for? How could it be that so many called, powerful, strong, intelligent and gifted people with a strong desire to be an entrepreneur repeatedly show up in one graveyard or the other to bury their dreams? At these graveyards we find ourselves engaging in an array of unequal trade transactions whereby we use the very same gifts and talents needed to succeed as an entrepreneur, to establish and sustain these organizations. Unfortunately, the sustenance of these organizations is done at the risk of suffocating our own dreams.

Now, I find myself pondering about the numerous world changers who the world never met, the trailblazers who never started and the giants who never woke up. I wonder if we are ever replaced, or will there be a perpetual gap for as long as we out of formation with our passion. The more I contemplate, the greater sense of urgency I feel to align myself in the order needed to serve according to the measures that were entrusted upon me.

CHAPTER FIVE

The Burial Procession

I've come to realize that the burial of the entrepreneur's dream is easily undetectable while showcasing the gifts, talents, creativity and leadership skills at the entrepreneur's graveyard. It is this diligence and dedication that have often led to promotion and elevation in a company. Before long, the promotion, the counterfeit wage increases and distorted upward mobility all have served to create a false sense of worth and validation. Without awareness, the entrepreneur now finds less time, less energy and less interest in pursuing what was once his or her passion, hope and path to freedom and generational wealth.

In fact, during the burial procession, many driven and ambitious entrepreneurs remained at the graveyard while still dreaming about entrepreneurship because they struggled to find the courage to detach themselves from the safety of employment. As an employed entrepreneur I served tirelessly as a high performer employee, because it was effortless to demonstrate the same leadership attributes as I would have exerted at my own establishment.

On the other hand, there are some entrepreneurs who chose to assimilate as a good employee after they have counted the C.O.S.T. Periodically, you will hear them share stories of their once living dream of entrepreneurship in the break room. Moreover, the assimilated entrepreneurs often take great effort to outline the benefits of becoming an employee as opposed to the benefits of pursuing entrepreneurship. I've also observed that the assimilated entrepreneur is often a model employee who is often not viewed as a threat, neither is this person intimidating because he or she is often viewed as an ideal non-confrontational employee.

Obviously, these series of events do not apply to all employed entrepreneurs. However, you will know you are in the number when you begin to recognize the pervasive discontent regardless of how high you climb the organizational chart. However, for many employed entrepreneurs, they learned the hard way that the endless hours of staying longer and working harder than others does not equate to any more job security than the employees who are mediocre.

The truth is that employed entrepreneurs are just as susceptible to the manipulation of "At Will" employment clause, lay-offs, and furloughs, even down to the final days before retirement. It is this truth that intensifies the pain as the doors revolve and the employed entrepreneurs observe the arrival of fresh blood who comes and also bury their dreams and others who are brave enough to leap before rigor-mortis sets in.

CHAPTER SIX

ITS TIME TO OWN IT

Over the years I've frequently heard the expression "don't count your chickens before they hatch". However, I beg you, when it comes to your journey to entrepreneurship, please **COUNT THEM**. See, it is customary to find ourselves attempting to explain the unexplainable desire to be an entrepreneur to people who don't deserve an explanation. And, because it is often unexplainable we may experience frustration because of all the ups and downs that comes with this process.

In essence, it makes sense to secure employment if we are lacking in funds; or, to ensure that the bills are paid and the immediate needs are met because we are taught at an early age to pursue an education and "get a good job" in order to succeed when we grow up. Needless to say, as a child it is very seldom that we are encouraged to "start a business" in order to succeed when we grow up. Therefore, this indescribable compelling desire to become an entrepreneur contradicts our upbringing and cultural norms.

As such, it is instinctual to fervently seek to secure another job if there is discontent of any sort; or, if we lose a job for any reason. Yet, we are not encouraged to continue on the path of entrepreneurship to perfect it if there is any discontent or if we fail at our attempts for any reason. In fact, in most cases, if an entrepreneur fails at any attempt, he/she is quickly reminded of all the reasons to seek employment instead of being encouraged to restructure and start again.

> *"Remember you still have to eat while you starting that little business"*
>
> *"Remember you still have bills to pay while you waiting for your business to grow"*

"Remember you still have mouths to feed while you waiting for the business to grow"

"Remember your kids still need a roof over their heads till that business takes off"

"I believe in your business idea but..."

"I just think you should work and save money while you're building your business on the side...."

"You have to be wise and realistic"

"I know but you need money in the meantime"

With this in mind, we must be forever mindful that it is not the responsibility of our family members or our employer to ensure that our dream comes alive. In fact, our employers hired us to perform because of our excellent skillset and it behoves them to hold on to us for as long as it serves them or assist them in attaining their goals. Thus, it is not their responsibility to empower us to thrive outside of the place of employment.

Therefore, our hunger to attain and succeed at entrepreneurship has to become personal. This is our calling, our dream, our passion, and our destiny, and this must remain our focus constantly. This may require frequent reflection on our personal "whys" and being cognizant of the fact no amount of failure is equivalent to the end of the journey, unless to permanently bury the dream. So, until we see the vision in all of its glory, we will need to own the responsibility to become until we own what we are becoming.

In other words, we will need to become totally committed to being our authentic self without deviation. Own the responsibilities of the CEO of your future establishment. Own the actions needed for the manifestation of the entrepreneurship dream. As horrible as this sounds, the truth is that our family members, spouses, friends and employers are being exactly who they are supposed to be. We're the ones that are out of formation and it is now time for us to become who we are supposed to be. So, it is time to own it until we are it. Own the journey, own the tears, own the losses and the wins. Own the process of becoming until we become.

CHAPTER SEVEN

IT'S BIGGER THAN YOU

I'm reminded of a very successful attorney who worked at a prestigious firm for twelve (12) years. After climbing the corporate ladder, she resigned suddenly in order to pursue her dream of opening her own bakery. She explained feeling as if she was failing her family; yet, described feeling free and fulfilled after she opened the bakery. She explained that going to law school made her family proud and "looked successful". She explained that neither her husband nor her family members bragged about her starting her own business until the bakery paid off the student loans and bought her mother a house.

This story has ignited a new level of understanding that in order for our entrepreneurship dreams to be manifested, stay alive or be revived, we must know without waiver that entrepreneurship is what we want without a plan B. This may require performing frequent self-inventory to determine whether or not any alternative to our entrepreneurship dreams is providing the same level of security, diversity and significance we intrinsically desire. Furthermore, we should perform self-inventory to determine whether or not any alternative to our entrepreneurship dreams is providing the same level of growth, impact and significance we intrinsically desire.

Nevertheless, I strongly believe that commitment to our entrepreneurial dreams are not only for our personal fulfillment; but, it is equally for the fulfilment of others around us. For example, in the end, the attorney informed me that becoming a baker and starting her own business allowed her to open doors for many people that she would not have been able to reach working at a prestigious law firm.

As a proud Jamaican, I love to proudly watch the Jamaican women winning the 4x 100 relay in the World Championship. I think about the significant role each woman plays in the passing of the baton to each other in order for the team to win. As such, Shelly-Ann Fraser-Pryce is faster than most discovered runners; yet, in the 4x 100 relay she is dependent on all the other runners. She needs them to hand her that baton in order for her to carry out her assignment as the Anchor in the race and take the baton over the finish line. This means there is an expectation for each runner to show up at the race and participate fully according to that which has been bestowed upon us because "To whom much is given, much will be required" (Luke 12:48). I can't help but wonder if there are any "Shelly-Ann Fraser-Pryce's" out there waiting, as an Anchor in life's relay, for me to pass them the baton.

Conclusion

Yes, there are many of us with powerful dreams and ambition to serve humanity via entrepreneurship, who took a different turn at the crossroad. For many, it may feel as if the dream will never be manifested and for some it looks impossible to get started. You have been contemplating giving up on that dream and plan to bury it at one entrepreneur's graveyard or the other. However, I believe that if you can't stop thinking about it, can't replace it and can't imagine the rest of my life without it, then you should pursue it.

See, for so many employed entrepreneurs, the dream keeps calling, it keeps taunting and no matter how much you have achieved or accomplished at the graveyard, it's hard to get it out of your mind. I recognize that doubt often intercept and fear shows up and does the rest; but, that's how we know we must fight to find a way to make this right because it could be the very thing that saves our lives and changes the entire trajectory of our lineage.

Even if you didn't make the right choice at the crossroad, it's not too late. Some things are worth fighting for, and your dream needs you to fight for it because there is someone waiting as an Anchor in life's 4x 100 relay to take the baton over the finish line. So right now, even with tears in your eyes, get up and fight for it. We cannot continue to bury this powerful desire to become a world changer at entrepreneur's graveyard. From this day on, we declare that we will be the generation with determination to make our inventions, to write and publish the bestselling books. We will paint the masterpieces and we refuse to bury the treasure of our full potential at the entrepreneur's graveyard.

"For the vision is yet for an appointed time, but at the end it shall speak, and not lie: though it tarry, wait for it; because it will surely come, it will not tarry".

Habakkuk 2:3 King James version

THANK YOU FOR READING

TIME TO REFLECT

1. Note any entrepreneurial dream that you have ever had:

2. Note any "side-chick" relationship you've had with your entrepreneurial dream:

3. Note the influential factors to engaging in any "side-chick" relationship with your entrepreneurial dream:

4. What were the motivating factors for wanting to become an entrepreneur?

5. Note any steps you have taken to initiate the birthing of your entrepreneurial dream:

6. Do you still have the dream of being an entrepreneur?

7. Including financial reward, what were some of the potential rewards of your entrepreneurial dream?

8. Aside from monetary gain; can the fulfillment you seek be found in a place other than entrepreneurship?

9. Was this worth giving up on my dreams?

ACKNOWLEDGEMENTS

How do I say thanks for all the things that God has done? While I do not have the words to express my eternal gratitude, I am fully conscious of the fact that all that I am or ever hope to become is because of His abundant provision and out pouring of His unending mercy. To my parents who made the ultimate sacrifice, I thank you without end. **DADDY** Rest in Peace, you protected me and with your stern reprimands and such incomprehensible love you taught me self-love and unique worthiness. As a young girl, you told me repeatedly that I was "comely".

Strangely enough, I didn't know what that word meant or understood what you were saying. Yet, during the times when I struggled most with my image and worth, I often heard your voice resonating in my ears over and over that I am "comely". At those moments, my spirit was always revived because of that soothing love that overfilled my heart because **DADDY SAID** I am comely. Now I know that you had chosen a unique word, for that time, to impress upon me that I am unique and beautiful. Thank you.

MOM, I often wondered if I am adopted because I could never understand how I could have been born to someone so calm, kind, nice, loving, God-fearing, and with such perseverance. I often dreamt of growing up and having those same qualities but in reality, know that I have such a long way to go. Thank you

To my children, Imraan and Imtiyaz Wise, I am always so thankful for having you both. I prayed for great children and God exceeded my expectations and blessed me with you both. I look at you both and I am reminded of the endless grace and mercy that's in my life. You are my constant reminder that God can and will do amazingly above and beyond what my mind has the ability to imagine. Therefore, I continue to imagine great things. Thank you both.

To my immediate family, my sister Dr. Jasmin Brown, my brothers Terrence, Rest in Peace, and Alan Brown, thank you all so much. I am so blessed to have family that has always supported and believed in my endeavors. I recognize that I have such a long way to go, but I want to assure you that I am on my way. Thank you.

To those who continue to believe in me and support all of my endeavors, (especially Minster Phyllis William and Minister Georgina Scott) thank you from the core of my heart. I want you to know that I love you more than words because you have always seen something great in me and continue to show me love when most wouldn't give even a prayer. I desire to make you so proud of me. Thank you!

To my good friends and supporters, thank you for sticking with me through the good, the bad and those unclear moments. I am not finished yet and the best is yet to come. Thank you.

Thank you

Made in the USA
Middletown, DE
06 October 2022

11984051R00029